The Journey Of Cancer

Camryn Hays

&

Bradi Keller

M. LiClar Publishing Co., LLC
Monroe City, MO

ISBN: 0997024763
ISBN-13: 978-0-9970247-6-0

IN MEMORY OF

DEDE YAGER
AND
DENNIS HANCOCK

1

There was a lady named Dede who had five children and 15 grandchildren. After teaching for several years, she loved spending her time making homemade noodles, reading to her grandchildren, going to her grandchildren's events, traveling, and praying. She was always thinking of other people by doing things such as cooking for them, visiting them, praying for them, and buying gifts well in advance.

In the same town of Monroe City, lived a man named Dennis. He had two children and three grandchildren. Dennis loved to make things out of wood, play basketball, help people learn to pole vault and play softball and spend lots of time with his grandkids.

There once came a day when Dede was diagnosed with breast cancer. A while later, Dennis was diagnosed with colon cancer. After many chemo treatments, Dede finally beat her cancer, but a couple years later her cancer came back a second time. Dennis and Dede ran into each other many times during chemo visits.

Dennis and Dede spent days in the hospital fighting and fighting. They even had surgeries to try to make the cancer go away. Their families came to visit them in the hospital. They made cards, prayed for them, and visited them to try to make them feel better.

When Dede was battling her cancer, then chemo made her lose her hair. She wore wigs and hats. Her grandchildren made her feel better by brushing her wigs for her. The chemo made her sick so she could not go and do a lot of things so her family would come to the house and sit with her.

Dede's children and grandchildren surprised her by making "Team Dede" shirts and spending the day together with her.

Dennis went through chemo too, but it affected him a little bit differently. He wasn't able to move around as much as before. He lost his hair also and didn't talk as much as he did before getting sick.. To make him feel better, his family would go get him strawberry shakes or other things to cheer him up.

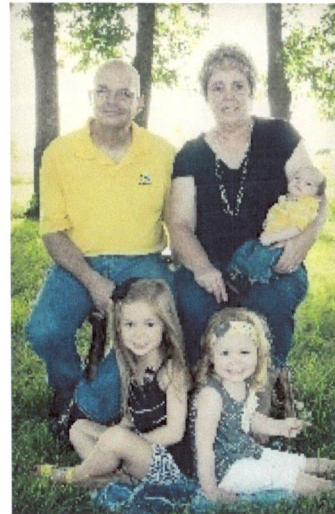

There once came a day when the doctors thought Dede had pneumonia. She spent a lot of time in the hospital trying to get better. Her husband Gary took her to a different hospital and they had to put a tube in her so she couldn't talk. At the end of the week, Dede went to be with Jesus. Now she is in a better place and doesn't hurt from the cancer. The next year, when it was Dede's birthday, some of her grandchildren brought balloons and cupcakes to her grave. They ate the cupcakes and released the balloons in the air by her grave.

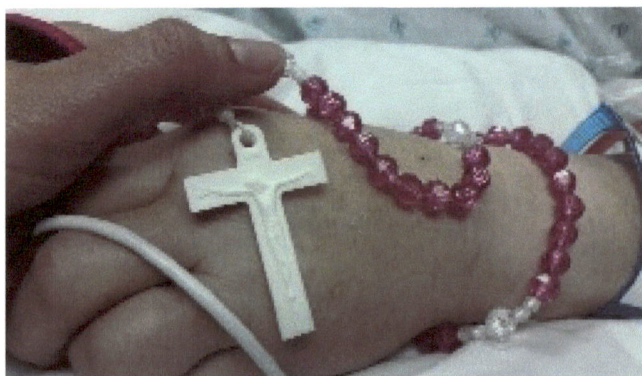

Dennis spent a lot of time in the hospital too, but then the doctors told him he could come home to be more comfortable. He had nurses that would come to his house to take care of him so he didn't have to stay in the hospital. One day, when everyone had left, Cindy, Dennis' wife, thought a nurse needed to be there. She called for the nurse and then Dennis went on to be with Jesus. He didn't want anyone to worry about him so we think that is why he waited for everyone to leave to go see Jesus.

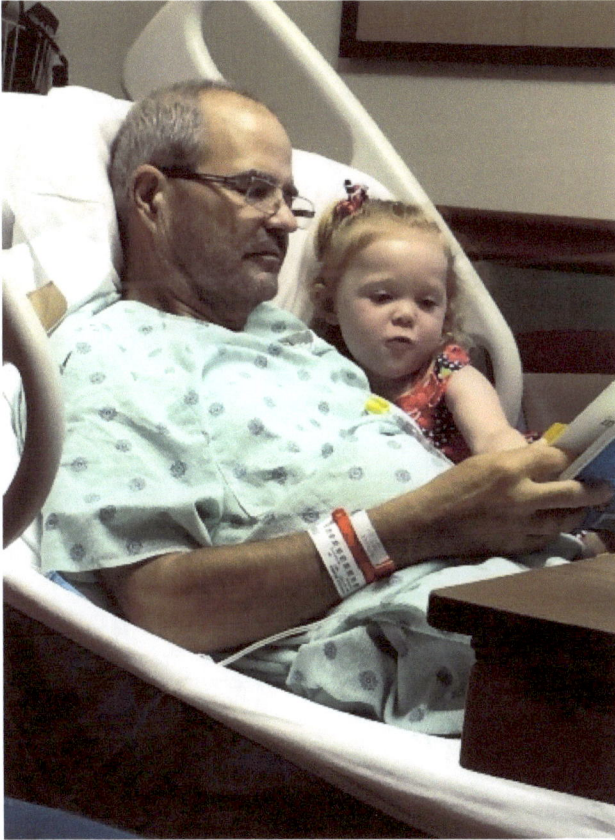

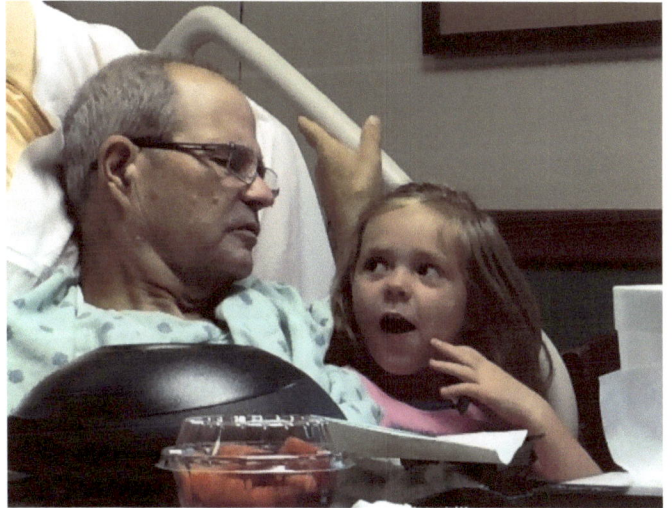

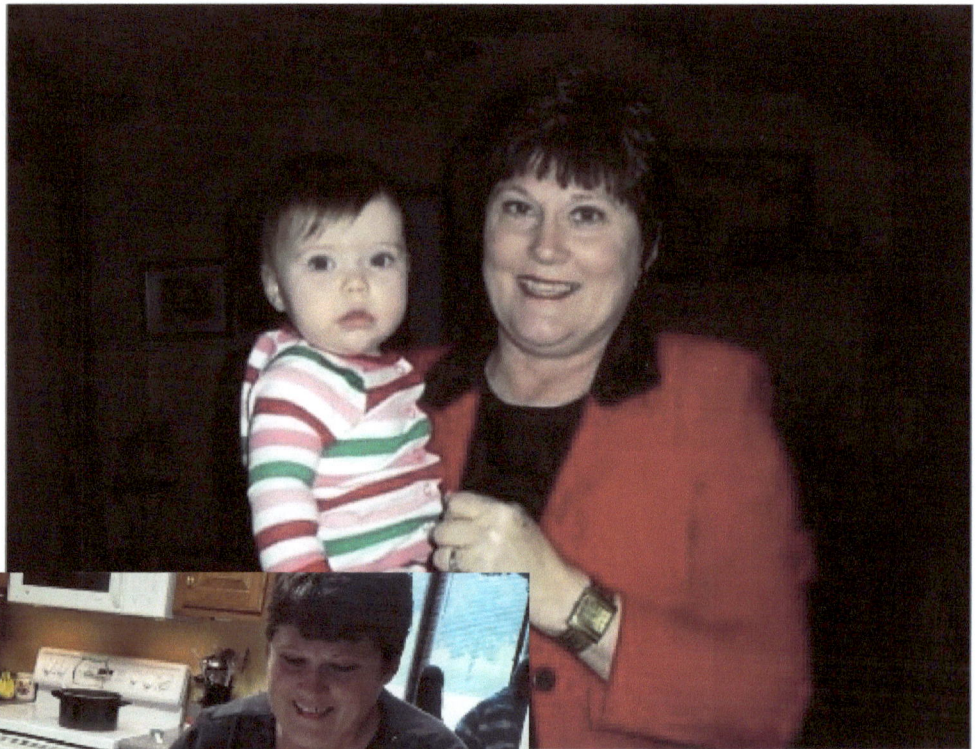

Dede and her
grandchild Camryn

Dede's grandchildren
and her loved making
homemade noodles.

Dennis and his grandchildren Bradi and Bella

Dennis and his wife and children

Dede's Family

Dennis' Family

TEAM DEDE
For Breast
Cancer
Awareness

Donkey Basketball

TEAM DENNIS
For Colon
Cancer
Awareness

When I was going through this hard time I stayed by family and friends and it helped me get through it. My family also prayed a lot with and for my grandma. So, if someone in your family has cancer stay by family and friends.

- Camryn Hays, granddaughter of Dede Yager

When I was going through this hard time I stayed with my family and friends in the hospital. It helped me get through the fear that everything would be ok. So, if someone in your family has cancer stay by family and friends.

- Bradi Keller, granddaughter of Dennis Hancock

ABOUT THE AUTHORS

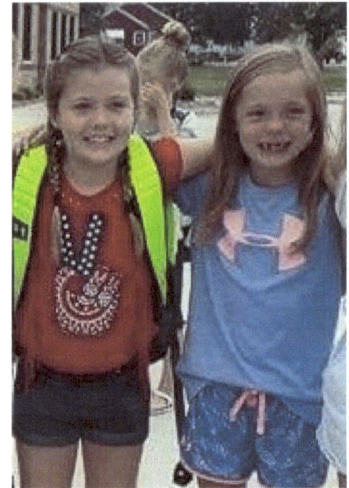

Camryn and Bradi are third grade classmates at Holy Rosary School. They have been friends since they met in kindergarten. The two of them share a bond as they both experienced the effects of cancer at the same time and lost a very special grandparent within a month of each other. They wanted to write this book to keep the memory of their grandparents alive and also share their journey for others experiencing cancer to realize they are not alone.

www.ingramcontent.com/pod-product-compliance
Lightning Source LLC
LaVergne TN
LVHW070347090426
835510LV00036B/92

9780099702476 0